Thrive! Endeavor®
All Thrive Forever®

by

Gary "Chris" Christopherson
Founder, *Thrive!*® - Building a Thriving Future
Founder, HealthePeople® - Building a Healthy and Thriving Future

Nelson, WI   University Park, MD

ISBN-13: 978-1512317237
ISBN-10: 1512317233

DEDICATION

People who help build, achieve and sustain
a surviving and thriving future for all forever.

Irene and Lynn Christopherson, nurturing and inspiring parents.
Dr. Patricia Haeuser, friend and supporter.

About The Author

Gary (Chris) Christopherson continues to work nationally and locally on improving health, reducing vulnerability and building a better future. Currently, he develops strategy, management and policy for creating, managing and sustaining large positive change and building a better and thriving future for all forever. ThrivingFuture.org He wrote the nonfiction books **Thrive! - Building a Thriving Future, Thrive! - People's Guide to a Thriving Future, The Thrive! Philosophy** and **Thrive! Endeavor** available via Amazon.com and ThrivingFuture.org.

Thrive! draws on his 30+ years experience creating, managing and sustaining large positive change at national and local levels in public and private sectors. He founded **HealthePeople** (building a healthy and thriving future; HealthePeople.com), *via*Future (creating large positive change) and **Vulnerable** (minimizing vulnerability). He served as a senior leader, manager and policymaker responsible for multi-billion dollar policy, programs and budgets and thousands of employees. His public service includes: Principal Deputy Assistant Secretary and Acting Assistant Secretary of Defense for Health Affairs and Senior Advisor, Department of Defense; Associate Director, Presidential Personnel, Executive Office of the President, White House; Senior Fellow, National Academy of Public Administration; Senior Advisor to Chief Operating Officer and Deputy Director for the Quality Improvement Group, Centers for Medicare and Medicaid Services, DHHS; Senior Advisor to Under Secretary, Veterans Health Administration, VA; Senior Fellow and Scholar-In-Residence, Institute of Medicine, National Academy of Sciences; Chief Information Officer, Veterans Health Administration, VA; Director of Health Legislation, House Select Committee on Aging, U.S. House of Representatives.

He is a sculptor of abstract art, focusing on Thrive! sculptures and creating over 150 sculptures. GChris Sculpture at GChris.com. He wrote science fiction novel **black box** and illustrated children's book **Angel, Thriving Creator of Artful Things**. Both are available via Amazon.com and GChris.com.

He received his bachelor's in political science and his master's in urban and regional planning from the University of Wisconsin – Madison, and did doctoral work in health policy and management at John Hopkins University School of Public Health.

Table of Contents

Summary
Thrive! Endeavor® (Tᴇ!)

A thriving and surviving future for you and all of us. We want and need it. We can achieve it. Now we are at the "tipping point" when our future is most endangered and we are most capable. You can build thriving future for yourself and help build thriving future for your communities and our world. What will you do?® The **Thrive! Endeavor®** (**Tᴇ!**) helps by motivating governments, private sector organizations and people of all backgrounds and generations to work together to build and sustain a thriving future.

What will your life and your world be in a thriving future where all survive and thrive forever, to the maximum extent possible? For you and your family and friends, you and your community, you and your country, and our world, a thriving future is a better life now and for the near and long term future. For you and all that you and we care about, it is a much better life and future with less vulnerability, with surviving and with sustained thriving.

Why must you and we care about a surviving and thriving future for you and your friends and family, your community, your country and our world? You and all of us want and need that future because of our endangered future and our human need to survive and desire to thrive. What drives us is that a person and a people need to survive and desire to thrive in the current and a sustainable future world.

Thrive! Survive! These are keys to a call for creating and sustaining large, positive and timely change and building a surviving and thriving future. *Thrive!*® (**T!**) is call to action and a rallying cry for a better and thriving future. *Thrive!*® is this future and is a bold vision and mission. To achieve that vision and succeed with the mission, the **Thrive! Endeavor®** (**Tᴇ!**), all of us together, strives to energize and empower people to build a thriving future for our families and friends, communities, countries and world. The **Endeavor** strives to build, achieve and sustain a surviving and thriving future for all forever.

Thrive! Endeavor® (TE!)
All Thrive Forever®

What the Thrive! Endeavor (TE!) is.

> What the **Thrive! Endeavor** is and strives to accomplish as the key mission of the overall *Thrive!*® strategy.

A thriving and surviving future for you and all of us. We want and need it. We can achieve it. Now we are at the "tipping point" when our future is most endangered and we are most capable.

You can build thriving future for yourself and help build thriving future for your communities and our world. What will you do? ®

The **Thrive! Endeavor® (TE!)** helps by motivating governments, private sector organizations and people of all backgrounds and generations to work together to build and sustain a thriving future.

Thrive!® (**T!**®) is aspiration, vision, mission and call to action. It is building, achieving and sustaining a surviving and thriving future for all forever.
- **T! Vision** is "All thrive forever. You, your communities, our world."
- **T! Mission** is "Create large, positive, timely change that achieves surviving and thriving future for all forever."
- **T! Strategy** is "A joint **Thrive! Endeavor** building a thriving future."

1

We can and should aspire to build, achieve and sustain a thriving future for all. Aspire to not only survive but thrive. Aspire individually and together to build a much better future. Aspire to thrive, achieving a thriving future for all forever.

Motivating us is the "human force", a large, positive and sustained driver of our behavior. Humans need to survive and desire to thrive today and forever. Humans have a unique desire to thrive. Humans have a unique ability and motivation to think through how to survive and thrive in the future.

Thrive! builds on our ability and desire to build a thriving future. Builds on a 1000+ year and 50+ generation strategy. Builds on "levers" and "fulcrums", enabling us to leverage our efforts to greater and long lasting outcomes. Builds on "tipping points", historical opportunities to make greater achievements. Builds on "next generation" strategies and tools. Builds on "eMedia" to expand reach and speed progress.

To build a thriving and surviving future, our joint and individual actions must avoid and reduce vulnerability and must increase surviving and thriving for all.
- What drives us is that people need to survive and desire to thrive.
- What should motivate us is the interests of both self and others and a much better near and far future.
- What enables us is our knowledge and tools (incl. **Thrive!** strategy and tools) which make us the most able in history.
- What is current historical tipping point is that our future is most endangered and we are most capable in history.

Which future do we choose and achieve?
- **Full Thrive (Best) Future – We change to "full thrive" path.** Thriving is high. Surviving and thriving are extended substantially beyond current path. <u>All</u> are performing well.
- Partial Thrive Future – We change to "partial thrive" path. There is more thriving. Surviving is extended beyond current

2

path. Compared to our current path, <u>more</u> are performing well.

- Survive Future – We change to "survive" path. Thriving is low. Surviving is extended beyond current path. Compared to what should be, too much of our world is performing poorly.
- **Current (Worst) Future** - We continue current path. Surviving and thriving are low. Surviving ends relatively soon. Compared to what should be, too much of our world is performing poorly.

Clearly, the best choice and the future we must achieve is the full thrive future.

To help you, your communities and our world survive and thrive, the **People's Guide to a Thriving Future [For All Forever]** is provided. It shows how to build a thriving future using **Thrive! Strategy and Action Plans**. It takes you through basics of building a thriving future along with detailed examples, worksheets and **Thrive! Next Generation Toolkit**. Available via <u>Amazon.com</u> or as free download @ <u>ThriveEndeavor.org</u>.

Now is the time for **Thrive!**, strategic advocacy for a thriving future for each and all of us. It is for the whole person, whole family, whole community, whole country and whole world. It is to move people from low to high ability, motivation, performance and status. It is strategic advocacy to move us all from vulnerability to surviving to thriving.

Thrive! Survive! Vulnerable! These are the keys to a call for creating and sustaining large, positive and timely change and building a surviving and thriving future. We are all vulnerable to some extent but that can change for the better. *Thrive!*® is call to action and a rallying cry for a better and thriving future. *Thrive!*® is this future and is a bold vision and mission.

To achieve that vision and succeed with the mission, the **Thrive! Endeavor**, all of us together, strives to energize and empower people to build a thriving future for our families and friends, communities, countries and world. The **Endeavor** strives to build,

3

achieve and sustain a surviving and thriving future for all forever, to the maximum extent possible. [See Table 1.]

Thrive!® (T!®) And Thrive! Endeavor® (TE!) Strategy Elements

T! Blogs:
- Key messages & suggested actions. ThriveBlog.org
- Challenges "What will you do?"® ThriveBlog.net

T! eMedia:
- **Linked** in **Thrive!** LinkedIn
- **f** **Thrive!** Facebook
- **Thrive!** Twitter
- **You Tube** **Thrive!** YouTube
- **t** **Thrive!** Tumblr

T! Websites:
- **Thrive! Endeavor®** ThriveEndeavor.org
- **All Thrive Forever®** AllThriveForever.org
- **Thrive! - Building a Thriving Future** ThrivingFuture.org
- **We Are Vulnerable** WeAreVulnerable.org
- **Thrive! - All Thrive Forever** ["Play game"] ThriveForever.org
- **HealthePeople®** HealthePeople.com
- **GChris Sculpture – Thrive! Sculpture** supports thriving. GChris.com

---

Table 1. Key *Thrive!* and **Thrive! Endeavor** strategy elements.

What a thriving future will be.

What your life and your world will be in a thriving future where all survive and thrive forever, to the maximum extent possible.

What will your life and your world be in a thriving future where all survive and thrive forever, to the maximum extent possible? *Thrive!*® is this future and is a bold vision and mission.

For you and your family and friends, a thriving future is a better life now and for the near and long term future for all of you and for future generations.

For you and your community, a thriving future is a better life now and for the near and long term future for the whole community and for all of the community's people.

For you and your country, a thriving future is a better life now and for the near and long term future for the whole country and for all of the country's people.

For our world, a thriving future is a better life now and for the near and long term future for the whole world (people and Earth, plants, animals, environment) and for all of the world's people and the Earth itself.

For you and all that you and we care about, it is a much better life and future with less vulnerability, with surviving and with sustained thriving.

When a surviving and thriving future is achieved, you, families and friends, communities, states, countries and the world will be:

- Performing well,
- Well-off (financially),
- Well nourished,
- Well housed,
- Well protected (exposures, crime),
- Well educated,
- Physically and mentally well (people),
- Growing/developing well,
- Living within good habitat,
- Physically well (Earth, plants, animals, environment),
- Not vulnerable,
- Producing personal and public goods,
- Living within a stable, positive climate, and
- Sustained.

When achieved, we will have helped you, families and friends, communities, states, countries and the world move up from:

- Performing poorly or badly,
- Being poor (financially),
- Being poorly nourished,
- Being poorly housed,
- Being poorly protected (exposures, crime),
- Being poorly educated,
- Being physically or mentally ill (people),
- Growing and developing poorly or badly,
- Not doing well "physically" (Earth, plants, animals, environment),
- Living within poor or bad habitat,
- Being excessively vulnerable,
- Living in an unstable, destructive climate, and
- Not being sustained.

When achieved, we will have fulfilled the hope of all, and especially:
- Vulnerable individual people (persons),
- Vulnerable families and friends,
- Vulnerable communities (including neighborhoods, villages, towns, cities, counties, regions),
- Vulnerable states,
- Vulnerable countries, and
- A vulnerable world.

When achieved, we will have:
- Thriving individual people (persons),
- Thriving families and friends,
- Thriving communities (including neighborhoods, villages, towns, cities, counties, states, regions),
- Thriving countries, and
- A thriving world.

Thrive!, a thriving future, is different and arguably better than anything tried or achieved in human history. Not just getting by or achieving a surviving future. A surviving future is necessary but not sufficient. It is a thriving future for all people and all future generations, a "50+ generation" strategy. Not just for some people or just for the current and next generation. It is a thriving future forever, a 1000+ year strategy. Not just for today or just 100 years. It is also for Earth on which we live and depend, not just for people.

Helping achieve this surviving and thriving future is the **Thrive! Endeavor**® - a vast human endeavor of you and all of us together striving for a surviving and thriving future. The **Thrive! Endeavor** strives for and envisions a surviving and thriving future, to the maximum extent possible, forever for all (you, family and friends, communities, countries and the world (including the Earth on which it depends).

Why care about a thriving future.

Why you and we must care about a surviving and thriving future for you. Your friends and family. Your community. Your country. Our world.

Why must you and we care about a surviving and thriving future for you and your friends and family, your community, your country and our world? You and all of us want and need that future because of our endangered future and our human need to survive and desire to thrive. What drives us is that a person and a people <u>need to survive</u> and <u>desire to thrive</u> in the current world and a sustainable future world.

Our needing and desiring a surviving and thriving future is driven by a natural human force - "a person needs to survive and desires to thrive." To truly satisfy this need and desire, we need the following:
1) we, as a person <u>and</u> a people, need to survive and desire to thrive,
2) we depend on <u>other persons</u> (a people) for survival and thriving, especially in the long term,
3) our need and desire applies to both the current <u>and</u> future world,
4) our <u>future</u> survival and thriving depends on there being a <u>future world</u>, and
5) our future world must be <u>sustainable</u> and <u>sustained</u> to fully meet our need and desire.

For these reasons, building, achieving and sustaining a thriving future forever (to the maximum extent possible) for you, your family and friends, your community, your country and our world is <u>the</u> human endeavor and <u>the</u> ideal.

9

This is why you and we care about a thriving future. But let's be a bit more specific.

What future must you and we build, achieve and sustain? You, your family and friends, your community, your country and our world want to and must build, achieve and sustain a surviving and thriving future.

All of us, almost without exception, want to thrive. Thriving means:
- Performing well,
- Being well-off (financially),
- Being well nourished,
- Being well housed,
- Being well protected (exposures, crime),
- Being well educated,
- Being physically and mentally well (people),
- Growing/developing well,
- Living within good habitat,
- Being physically well (Earth, plants, animals, environment),
- Not being vulnerable,
- Producing personal and public goods,
- Living within a stable, positive climate, and
- Being sustained.

This is the best future for you, your family and friends, your community, your country and our world (including the Earth on which we depend).

All of us, almost without exception, want to and must survive. Surviving means at least:
- Performing at a minimal level,
- Having the minimum levels of resources, food, housing, protection, education, physical and mental health (people), personal growth and development, and habitat,
- Surviving "physically" (Earth, plants, animals, environment),
- Not being excessively vulnerable,
- Producing minimum levels of personal and public goods,
- Being in an humanly survivable climate, and
- Being sustained at a minimal survival level.

This is not the best future but it is far better than not surviving.

What future must we avoid? You, your family and friends, your community, your country and our world want to and must <u>avoid a bad or endangered future</u>. A bad future means:

- Performing poorly or badly,
- Being poor (financially),
- Being poorly nourished,
- Being poorly housed,
- Being poorly protected (exposures, crime),
- Being poorly educated,
- Not being physically or mentally well (people),
- Not growing and developing well,
- Not doing well "physically" (Earth, plants, animals, environment),
- Living within poor or bad habitat,
- Being excessively vulnerable,
- Living in an unstable, destructive climate, and/or
- Not being sustained.

In an endangered future, there is the risk of any or all of these. No one wants to risk this bad future let alone live this bad future.

A bad future also means not fixing what we already know is broken and likely to stay broken.

As we look around us at the people and the world which we care about, much of what is important to us is already broken or is endangered, much of it unnecessarily so. This is probably true for you and your family. This is true for your community, your country and our world.

For example, in the United States, our financial systems' failure did and still could bring down countries' and the world's financial system. Housing bubbles have burst and lifetime savings lost. While some of our housing markets improve, many people cannot buy homes (lack resources, can't get loans, job insecurity) or they own homes they cannot afford or sell. Even with the Affordable

Care Act, our health care remains inaccessible, unaffordable and of poor quality for many people. Our education systems leave children behind and fail to educate children to their full potential. Our economic system rewards many people far beyond their contribution, holds many far below their potential contribution, and keeps many in or near poverty. Our environment is under more stress than it can handle in the decades and centuries to come. On energy, our future was bet on non-renewable energy sources and we have yet to turn to conservation and renewable energy at a level commensurate with long term energy needs and supply.

For some countries, the situation is better. For some, it is worse. All countries and the world as a whole are and will continue to be broken to some greater or lesser extent.

But these are only individual broken pieces for us to fix. In the real world, fixing the future means fixing these broken pieces together with fixing related broken pieces, e.g. health with the economy, education with food, energy with the environment, and housing with protection. Fixing these together is more likely to achieve a surviving and thriving future. Fixing all of these together is the most likely to achieve a thriving future.

Because it is people who have broken much of the world and endangered its future, it is people who must care about and must fix what is broken and build a survivable and thriving future. Because it is only people who can change our future, it is people who must build, achieve and sustain a surviving and thriving future.

All of this is why you and we care about a surviving and thriving future. This is the reason for the **Thrive! Endeavor**®.

How the Thrive! Endeavor (Tᴇ!) builds a thriving future.

> How the *Thrive!* **Endeavor**, you and all of us together, builds, achieves and sustains <u>a thriving future</u> <u>for all</u> <u>forever</u>.

Thrive! Survive! Vulnerable! These are the keys to a call for creating and sustaining large, positive and timely change and building a surviving and thriving future. We are all vulnerable to some extent but that can change for the better. *Thrive!*® is that call to action and a rallying cry for a better and thriving future. It is a vision and a mission for those wanting to build a better future. To achieve that vision and succeed with the mission, the **Thrive! Endeavor**®, all of us together, strives to energize and empower people to build a thriving future for our families and friends, communities, countries and world. It strives to build, achieve and sustain a surviving and thriving future for all forever, to the maximum extent possible.[1] **Thrive!** is this future and is a bold vision and mission.

Earlier, we laid out why build a surviving and thriving future for you and your family and friends, you and your community, you and your country, and you and our world. But to truly have a thriving future, we need to have it for you and <u>everybody's</u> family and friends and <u>every</u> community and <u>every</u> country and <u>every part of and our entire</u> world. When all this comes together, you and all of us will have built, achieved and sustained a surviving and thriving future.

---

[1] We must keep in mind that "our world" and "all" is expanding as we explore and move beyond earth to other parts of our universe. For that reason, "a thriving future for all forever" reaches as far as we reach or hope to reach.

13

How best to do this? We bring all this together with the **Thrive! Endeavor** where you and all of us together, build, achieve and sustain <u>a thriving future</u> <u>for all</u> <u>forever</u>.

Why the Thrive! Endeavor?

As laid out earlier, you and all of us want and need a surviving and thriving future because of our endangered future and our human need to survive and desire to thrive. And <u>only people</u> can and must fix all that is broken. And <u>only people</u> can and must build, achieve and sustain a survivable and thriving future. And <u>only all of us joined together</u> can succeed due to the scope (all), level (surviving and thriving), duration (forever) of the challenge. For these reasons, building, achieving and sustaining a surviving and thriving future requires a vast, sustained **Endeavor** of all of us together.

What is the Thrive! Endeavor?

The **Endeavor** is all of us together. It is vision, mission, strategy and call to action. Its vision is a surviving and thriving future for all forever. Its mission is to create and sustain large positive and timely change that builds, achieves and sustains a surviving and thriving future for all forever, to the maximum extent possible. Its strategy is to energize and empower all of us together in the vast, sustained human endeavor building and sustaining a thriving future. Its call for action is to motivate all of us (individual people, groups of people, private sector organizations, governments) to seek a thriving future, to create and sustain the necessary large positive change, and to work together to build, achieve and sustain a surviving and thriving future.

In support of this vision and mission, the Endeavor adopts and embraces "**A People's Constitution**" - "We the people, in order to form a more perfect union, commit to a thriving future for all forever." [2]

Who is and will be the Thrive! Endeavor?

The **Endeavor** is <u>all of us together</u> building, achieving and sustaining a surviving and thriving future. "All of us together" include individual people, groups of people, private sector organizations and governments. "All of us together" include <u>current and future generations</u>. "All of us together" include <u>you</u>, and <u>everybody's</u> family and friends, and <u>every</u> community, and <u>every</u> country, and <u>every part of and our entire</u> world.

Who does what and how in the Thrive! Endeavor?

What the **Endeavor** does and how it does it is different than past and current approaches which have major limitations and defects. The **Endeavor** is unique and better because it:

- Strives to achieve a thriving and sustainable future for all forever, to the maximum extent possible. But it also helps ensure survival, a necessary but not sufficient step to achieving a thriving future
- Enables the building of a surviving and thriving future for you, your family and friends, your community, your country and our world.
- Joins people of all backgrounds/generations together to achieve a thriving future.
- Is able to address every person, community and issue.
- Uses whole "community" (local, regional, state, country, world/global) strategy for creating and sustaining change and building thriving futures. [No longer should we rely on piecemeal strategies.]

---

[2] The **People's Constitution** should be just this brief, understandable and powerful. It should not replace any country's constitution. The intent is for it to be embraced by and acted upon affirmatively by all people forever.

- Uses whole "person" strategy for creating and sustaining change and building thriving futures. [No longer is the focus only on parts (ill health, hunger, poor education or insufficient income).]
- Uses whole "system" (community, health, education, economy, housing, etc.) strategy for creating and sustaining change and building thriving futures. [No longer should we rely on survival and piecemeal strategies for just parts of a system.]
- Takes an integrated approach to cross-cutting issues.
- Uses an integrated approach to people/environment strategy, change and thriving futures. [No longer is the focus only on people or the environment.]
- Uses a "person-centered" strategic approach that recognizes people's behaviors are the problem and the solution. [No longer should we fail to address "people's behavior".]
- Uses eMedia and social networking to expand communication and joint action and to activate and coordinate a large endeavor in "real time".
- Uses the **Thrive! Next Generation Toolkit** [contained in the full **Thrive! - People's Guide To A Thriving Future [For All Forever** available via ThriveEndeavor.org and Amazon.com] of strategy, models and tools to create and sustain change and build thriving futures. [No longer should we rely on past approaches that failed or had limited success.]
- Uses strategic/operational planning and combines it with strategic/operational management and execution.
- Creates a collaborative strategy with the necessary positive actions to build, achieve and sustain a surviving and thriving future.

To improve our chances of success, the **Endeavor** recognizes and will positively use tipping points, a critical element in positive change efforts historically.[3] Throughout human history, we see moments when "tipping points" exist. Tipping points can help enable negative or positive change. We see moments when a positive action is taken at a tipping point and major positive change occurs. We are now at such a tipping point. We are now at an historical moment when government and the private sector are broken in many ways, when our resources are becoming increasingly limited, when our environment is increasingly and negatively impacted, when our future is endangered, and when a failure to act positively dooms us to a failed, potentially non-survivable future. But, it is also a historical moment when we are the most able to change all that for the better. At this tipping point when our future is most endangered and we are most able, carefully developed and positive actions are more necessary and more likely to be effective and successful.

Each and all of us should develop and take as many positive actions as we can. The more positive actions taken, the better for all of us. Each and all of us should help build, achieve and sustain a surviving

---

[3] Using tipping points can be very helpful in building a thriving future. However, positive change efforts can also occur without an existing or future tipping point and without creating a tipping point. It is just more difficult. Where feasible, we should use existing, future and creatable tipping points:

- Use current tipping points.
- Partner with families and friends, communities and countries that are broken and/or with clearly endangered futures.
- Partner with families and friends, communities and countries that are positioned to move up from surviving to thriving.
- Build off issue areas and cross-cutting issue areas that are broken and/or with endangered futures.
- Use breakthroughs in knowledge and technology.
- Partner with new, more capable and more motivated leaders emerge.
- Use eMedia and social networking.
- Use grassroots and self-organizing movements.
- Watch for and use new tipping points as they emerge.
- When necessary, appropriate and doable, create new tipping points that are opportunities to build a thriving future.

and thriving future for <u>our family and friends</u>. Each and all of us should help build, achieve and sustain a surviving and thriving future for <u>our community</u>. Each and all of us should help build, achieve and sustain a surviving and thriving future for <u>our country</u>. Each and all of us should help build, achieve and sustain a surviving and thriving future for <u>our world</u>, including the Earth on which we depend. Via these actions and the **Endeavor**, <u>each and all of us together</u> should build, achieve and sustain a surviving and thriving future.

What positive actions are needed to bring about the needed changes that improve our current status enough to achieve the desired surviving and thriving status? [Figure 1. Building a Thriving Future.] Each and all of us identify actions that support <u>good</u> changes that will help reduce vulnerability and/or improve and/or sustain surviving and thriving. If good changes are likely to occur, together we support them. If good changes are not likely to occur, together we support them and develop other good changes to compensate.

Each and all of us identify actions that stop <u>bad</u> changes that increase vulnerability and/or prevent or limit surviving and thriving. If bad changes are not likely to occur, together we ensure they do not. If bad changes are likely to occur, together we change them, stop them or avoid/reduce their impact.

Via the **Endeavor**, all of us together develop our strategy and successfully take the actions to ensure a surviving and thriving future.

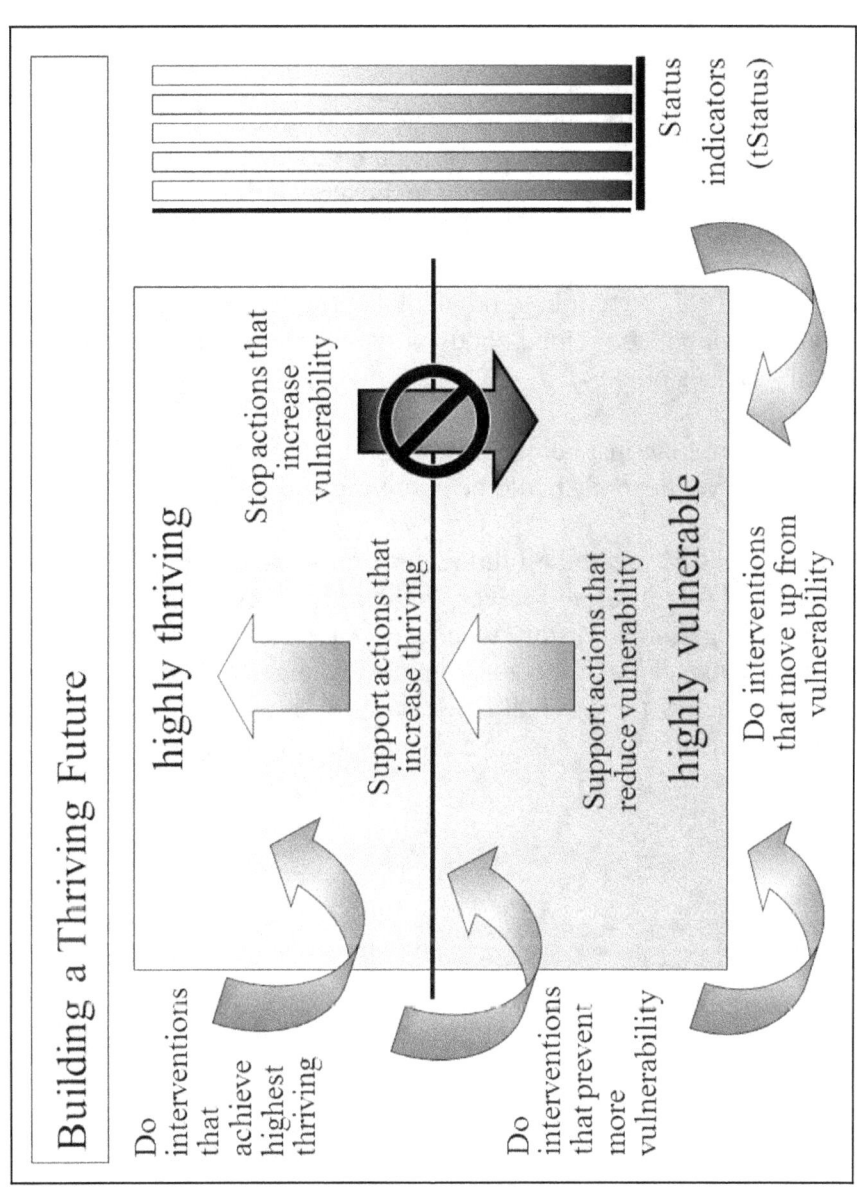

Figure 1. Building a Thriving Future.

19

With what result?

When successful, all of us, current and future, should be performing well. Be well-off (financially). Be well nourished (food and drink). Be well housed. Be well protected (exposures, crime). Be well educated. Be physically and mentally well (people). Personally grow/develop well. Be physically well (Earth, plants, animals, environment). Live within good habitat. Not be vulnerable. Produce personal and public goods. Live within a stable, positive climate. Be sustained.

But it is more than just people surviving and thriving. The Earth upon which we depend should be surviving and thriving.

When successful, we and all future generations achieve the surviving and thriving future for all forever, to the maximum extent possible. At this time in human history when we desire to thrive, when we need to survive, when our future is most endangered, and when we are most capable, the **Thrive! Endeavor**, all of us together, can and must build, achieve and sustain a thriving future for all forever.

www.ingramcontent.com/pod-product-compliance
Lightning Source LLC
Chambersburg PA
CBHW072253310526
45795CB00011B/1094